Digital Mindfulness
Cultivating Better Mental Health Online

Table of Contents

Chapter 1. Introduction

Welcome to a journey that marries the ancient practice of mindfulness with the dynamic landscape of the digital world. Our Special Report on "Digital Mindfulness: Cultivating Better Mental Health Online" illuminates a new path to mental well-being in the increasingly complex online universe. This isn't about technical complexities, but a beautifully simple blend of traditional wisdom and contemporary science crafted to inspire, motivate, and guide you towards maintaining healthier relationships with your digital companions. Grasp this compelling opportunity to discover how digital platforms can become tools for tranquility, fostering rather than hindering your mental health. With insights backed by esteemed mental health professionals, technology experts and mindfulness practitioners, this report has the potential to revolutionize your digital experience. Give yourself this blissful gift of revelation; because a better digital life with enriched mental health is just a few pages away.

Chapter 2. Embracing Digital Mindfulness: An Introduction

Mindfulness, a practice with roots in ancient Buddhist philosophy, can help train our attention for the real-time awareness of our thoughts, feelings, and surrounding environment. This level of present moment attention can lead to improvements in mental well-being, stress reduction, increased focus, and more. In the age of ubiquitous digital technology, however, achieving this kind of mindfulness can be challenging. The constant notifications, endless social media feeds, and ease of access to any number of distractions can derail our efforts and lead to feelings of disenchantment with our digital lives.

2.1. The Landscape of Digital Distractions

We are living in an era marked by increasing digitization. Our smartphones serve as gateways to vast, interconnected virtual worlds filled with information, entertainment, social networks, and professional opportunities. Yet, this digital abundance also introduces several challenges – a never-ending cascade of emails, social media updates, and disruptions that fragment our attention and eclipse the focus required for deep thinking and mindfulness.

Our brains are biologically wired to respond to these new stimuli. Researchers believe this stems from our evolutionary survival instinct, where noticing and reacting to a new element in the environment could mean the difference between life and death. In the modern digital jungle, however, these responses often lead to pattern interrupts and a state of chronic distractibility.

2.2. Meeting Mindfulness

Mindfulness, rooted in far-eastern philosophies, has received widespread acceptance and validation in the western psychology paradigm in recent decades. It is essentially the capacity to focus attention on the present moment, with a kind, non-judgmental attitude. Mindfulness allows you to observe your thoughts and feelings from a distance, without letting them control you.

Practicing mindfulness offers a gateway to tranquility in our chaotic digital age. It can aid us in retaining control over our attention, fostering deeper connections with others, practicing empathy and compassion, reducing stress, and enhancing our overall well-being.

2.3. Digital Mindfulness: A Marriage of Antiquity and Technology

Bearing this, an evolution of mindfulness practice is being observed – one that does not suggest a complete disconnection from digital technologies but encourages a more conscious, mindful approach towards them. Referred to as 'Digital Mindfulness,' it aspires to adapt the principles of mindfulness within a digital context.

Instead of combatting technology with attempts to escape or reject it, digital mindfulness encourages the use of technology in a way that promotes focus, productivity, and mental well-being. It involves designing and using digital tools mindfully, such that they help users bring their awareness back to the present moment rather than pulling it away. This science-driven, practical approach could transform our digital interactions from sources of stress to platforms for enhancing mental health.

2.4. The Case for Digital Mindfulness

While the internet and digital platforms offer unprecedented opportunities to learn, create, and connect, evidence suggests that excessive use may contribute to mental health issues such as anxiety, depression, loneliness, ADHD, and more. Many users struggle with the compulsion to check emails, social media profiles, or the urge to stay 'connected' constantly. Within these patterns, the importance of implementing digital mindfulness becomes clear.

Adopting digital mindfulness allows us to make informed, conscious decisions about how and when we use technology and the internet, encouraging healthier patterns of use. By recognizing the potential impacts of our digital behaviors – both beneficial and detrimental – we can make active choices about how to maintain balance in our digital lives.

2.5. Techniques for Embracing Digital Mindfulness

Adopting digital mindfulness involves both changes to our behaviors and our tools. It requires creating digital environments that support our well-being and align with our intentions, and harnessing the power of our minds to control the way we interact with technology.

1. It starts with awareness: Begin by observing your behavior around technology. How often do you check your smartphone? Are your online activities positively contributing to your well-being and goals? Bring an attitude of curiosity to this self-exploration.

2. Intentionally unplug: Establish times for taking a break from the digital world. Unplugging allows your mind to reset, reducing stress, and promoting feelings of groundedness.

3. Use technology to support your mindfulness practice: Numerous

apps offer guided meditations, breathing exercise prompts, and reminders to take breaks from screen time. You can leverage these tools to enhance your mindfulness practice.

4. Design for attention: Refine your digital spaces. This includes clearing unnecessary apps and notifications from your phone, using plugins to block distracting websites, and creating physical zones free from digital interruptions.

By mastering this strategy, we can transform our relationships with the digital platforms that are integral to our way of life, making them contribute positively to our overall mental well-being.

2.6. The Path Forward

As we continue on this exploration of digital mindfulness, we will delve deeper into various aspects of mindful tech-use. We'll study different mindfulness techniques and tools, discuss how to create a healthier digital environment, and explore in detail the impact of our digital behaviors on our mental health. We're at the forefront of the mindfulness revolution, where the shift toward a more conscious, intentional use of technology awaits us. A world of digital serenity lies ahead; we just need to embrace it mindfully and march forward.

Chapter 3. Impact of Digital Media on Mental Health

In the heartlands of the modern world, the Digital Age has firmly taken root, creating an unprecedented revolution in information access. From social media platforms to news websites, digital technologies have pervasively infiltrated every corner of our lives. These digital avenues, while facilitating connectivity, convenience, and access to virtually unlimited amounts of data, also possess profound implications on mental health.

3.1. The Rise of Digital Consumption

An astonishing majority of human lives have been significantly technology-infused in the recent past. A study by the Royal Society for Public Health in 2017 found that young people spend an average of over four hours online daily. The omnipresence of digital media impels us to remain connected, often at the cost of our peace of mind.

3.2. The Constant Buzz: Connectivity or Overwhelm?

One of the substantial consequences of this entangled interface is the expectation to be continuously connected and responsive. This relentless buzz of notifications can create an overwhelming sense of obligation and anxiety. Our brain's dopamine-driven reward system is also manipulated by the desire to feel included and acknowledged. Thus, we constantly check for updates, likes, and shares, entrapping us into a cycle of digital hyperconnectivity that often leads to anxiety and stress.

3.3. The Comparison Culture: The Social Media Cycle

Social networking sites have given rise to a new type of self-esteem based on the perception and validation from others. Through perfectly curated posts showcasing idealized images of beauty, success, and happiness, the online sphere has become a ground for comparison. The constant striving toward impossibly perfect standards can result in lowered self-esteem, isolation, and in severe instances, depression and body dysmorphic disorders.

3.4. Digital Media: Fuelling FOMO

FOMO, or the "fear of missing out," is a phenomenon that compels us to incessantly check social media to ensure we're up-to-date and included in shared experiences. FOMO can create anxiety, disrupt sleep patterns, and lead to emotional instability. It forcefully projects a constant need to be in the loop of every social incidence, escalating levels of stress and dissatisfaction.

3.5. Cyberbullying: The Dark Corner of Digital Spaces

With anonymity and lack of regulation, the digital world also harbors cyberbullying. Virtual bullying can lead to traumatizing effects, such as depression, anxiety, self-harm, and in extreme cases, suicide. Statistics reveal the disturbing extent to which this has become a global issue, with 37% of young people admitted having experienced cyberbullying on a personal level.

3.6. The Blue Light Effect: Disrupting Sleep

Another deleterious impact of digital media overuse is the "blue light" effect, disrupting our sleep patterns. Exposure to screens close to bedtime delays the release of sleep-inducing melatonin, increases alertness, and resets the internal body clock, leading to disrupted sleep schedules. Chronic sleep disruptions can accelerate various mental health issues, including anxiety and depressive disorders.

3.7. Information Overload: Cognitive Overwhelm

Our brains are bombarded with large volumes of digital information daily, leading to cognitive overload. Constant processing of a vast amount of data can cause mental fatigue and stress, impairing decision-making capabilities, focus, and creativity.

However, the digital media environment isn't entirely bleak. It offers opportunities for users to harness its robust platforms for mindfulness practices and improved mental health, provided they apply a conscious approach to digital consumption.

3.8. Digital Mindfulness: Making the Shift

By integrating practices like setting dedicated digital-free hours, mindful "digital dieting", and using tech tools to promote mindfulness, we can transform our digital interactions into a path of tranquility. Be it through digital detox, meditation apps, or virtual therapy, the possibilities for cultivating digital mindfulness are as expansive as the digital universe.

While the digital landscape's impacts on mental health are substantial, the keys to mitigating the adverse effects are in our hands. By adopting a mindful approach to digital media interactions, we can make our digital journey a source of positivity, connection, and well-being. This digital-space navigation is more about balance, less about despair; more about mindfully interacting with technology, less about falling prey to its incessant demands. It is indeed possible to foster a harmonious relationship with our digital companions, where mental health and digital consumption co-exist, enriching each other rather than cancelling out.

Chapter 4. The Concept of Mindfulness: A Comprehensive Understanding

The concept of mindfulness, a seemingly simple but actually complex and multifaceted phenomenon, has witnessed a surge of interest in contemporary society. While some may erroneously dismiss mindfulness as a mere trend of sorts, it is, in fact, a time-honored practice deeply rooted in various philosophical, religious, and cultural traditions worldwide.

4.1. Origins and Definitions

The origins of mindfulness can be traced back to ancient times. Notably, it holds a significant place in Buddhism, where it is conceptualized as Sati. Sati, or mindfulness, is one of the seven factors of enlightenment in the Theravada tradition and is essentially about clear awareness. The Pali canon, an ancient Buddhist scripture, defines it as the ability to remember, suggesting a keeping in mind of what has been done and said.

But mindfulness goes beyond Buddhist philosophy. It resonates with philosophies and practices in many religions and cultures, including Christianity, Taoism, and Yoga philosophies, among others.

In the modern context, mindfulness has been defined variously but usually involves paying attention in a particular way. An often-cited definition is that by Kabat-Zinn, who describes mindfulness as "paying attention in a particular way: on purpose, in the present moment, and non-judgmentally."

Yet another definition by Bishop et al. conceptualizes mindfulness as a two-component model: self-regulation of attention maintained on immediate experience and adopting a specific orientation that is characterized by curiosity, openness, and acceptance.

4.2. Philosophical Underpinnings

A notable driving force behind the rising interest in mindfulness in the Western world can be traced to the work of Jon Kabat-Zinn. Particularly, his Mindfulness-Based Stress Reduction (MBSR) programme, developed at the University of Massachusetts Medical School in the 1970s, combined mindfulness practices, particularly meditation and yoga, with Western psychology and medicine, generating a significant impact across various domains of society, including healthcare, education, and corporate environments

Kabat-Zinn's philosophical stand was heavily influenced by Buddhism, and he took great strides to decontextualize mindfulness from its religious origins, cultivating a secular approach that could be widely accepted in a clinical context. This modified version of mindfulness, often termed 'secular mindfulness,' has been integral to its acceptance and application in the Western world.

4.3. Understanding Mindfulness Practice

While mindfulness may be perceived as an overarching concept, at its core, it's about the practice, which includes mindfulness meditation. Essentially, this practice involves focusing one's attention on the present moment without drifting into concerns about the past or future or getting swayed by distracting thoughts.

The basic tenets include mindfulness breathing, body scan, and mindful observation, among others, all of which nurture a strong sense of presence. For example, in mindfulness breathing, one focuses on the breath, noticing each inhale and exhale without trying to change the breathing pattern.

4.4. The Neuroscience of Mindfulness

Understanding the neuroscience of mindfulness can underscore its effectiveness in promoting well-being. Neuroscientific research into mindfulness reveals several significant effects on the brain.

Some of the key areas the practice impacts include the prefrontal cortex associated with executive functioning, the anterior cingulate cortex linked with self-regulation, and the hippocampus, which plays a crucial role in memory formation and retrieval. These changes translate into improved attention and focus, better emotional regulation, and enhanced cognitive flexibility.

4.5. Mindfulness in the Digital Age

We live in a world dominated by digital technology, and the rapid pace and information overload can feel overwhelming. This need to constantly stay 'connected' can give rise to stress, fatigue, and a sense of disorientation, creating a distance from our 'self'. This is where mindfulness can play a vital role.

Digital mindfulness means integrating mindfulness into our online behaviors to craft a more balanced and healthy relationship with technology. It's about conscious consumption of technology, controlling the narrative of our digital experiences, and being present in our online interactions.

In summary, the concept of mindfulness embodies a dynamic blend of age-old wisdom and contemporary science. It's not about the passive acceptance of reality, but an active process of connecting with the self and the world in a more meaningful and thoughtful way. Its beneficial impact spans from cognitive and emotional improvements to enhanced well-being and productivity, which holds even more relevance in our increasingly digital reality. As such, integrating mindful practices as part of our digital behavior can lead to more controlled, authentic, and rewarding online experiences.

Chapter 5. Digital Chaos to Digital Calm: The Power of Mindfulness

Surrounded by beeps, pings, and frantic scrolling, our minds become saturated in a cacophony of digital stimuli. This overload drowns out the silence required for introspection and deeper connections with ourselves and the world around us. So how do we find calm within this chaos? The answer lies in blending the cerebral art of mindfulness with our digital interactions.

==⬜Understanding the Digital Chaos⬜⬜

The term "Digital Chaos" refers to the overwhelming flurry of digital stimuli that we experience daily. If left unchecked, this can lead to stress, anxiety, burnouts, and a profound sense of disconnection from the real world.

According to the American Psychiatric Association, prolonged exposure to Digital Chaos can profoundly impact mental health. Consequently, it is crucial to thoroughly understand this concept to combat it effectively.

==⬜Countering Digital Stressors⬜⬜

Coping strategies for digital stressors range from limiting screen time to using technology mindfully. These approaches demand us to question our compulsions and implicitly challenge our existing relationship with technology.

With increasing volumes of information vying for our attention, our mental resources are often pushed to their limits. A comprehensive strategy to rehabilitate our digital habits involves a mixture of awareness, regulation, and the construction of tech-positive habits.

5.1. Creating Awareness

Awareness marks the starting point of this journey. Remaining oblivious to the quantities of digital information we consume or the time we spend online will only fuel the chaos. Here, digital mindfulness begins with self-questioning: How much time do you spend on digital platforms? How does it affect your emotional health, productivity, social life, and physical well-being? Honest responses guide us towards mindful engagement with technology.

===Regulating Digital Interactions

Regulation flows from awareness. It involves setting personal boundaries on digital usage based upon the insights gathered through self-questioning. You might schedule specific 'digital detox' periods, opt for tech-free zones at home, or limit notifications to essential apps only. This stage calls for an explicit commitment to redefining and maintaining healthier digital routines.

5.2. Constructing Tech-Positive Habits

Building on awareness and regulation, tech-positive habits are about leveraging tech tools that enhance emotional and mental health. This could mean using apps that promote mindfulness, cognitive-behavioral therapy, sleep hygiene, physical activity, etc. The goal is to shift from mindless to mindful consumption of digital content, fostering a digitally nourished, balanced life.

== The Role of Mindfulness

While strategies to combat digital stressors may differ, a common thread ties them all: mindfulness. Mindfulness is an ancient practice grounded in being intensely aware of what you're sensibly experiencing in the present moment, without interpretation or judgment.

Integrating mindfulness into our digital habits doesn't mean eschewing technology; instead, it's about fostering a more gracious, purposeful, and measured relationship with it.

===□Benefiting From Mindful Scrolling

To scroll is human; to scroll mindfully is divine. Mindful scrolling involves fully grasizing each piece of information we consume, thus tackling the infamous "scrolling syndrome". This radically differentiates the quality, quantity, and caliber of data consumed.

5.3. Mindful Messaging and Posting

The mindfulness paradigm proposes a conscious intent behind every digital interaction, be it messaging or social media postings. It asks: "What is my intention behind this message/post?" This simple question challenges us to think before digital broadcasting, promoting healthier digital communication that is alignment with our inner values and convictions.

Chapter 6. From Chaos to Calm: The Real-World Impact□□

The real-world implications are transformative. Better digital habits contribute to reduced stress levels, fewer instances of screen-induced headaches, healthier sleep patterns, and more engaging social interactions.

These benefits seep into other aspects of our lives as well - healthier work boundaries, a sharpened focus, and balanced leisure time. Ultimately, applying mindfulness to your digital world opens up an entirely new way of life, potentially fostering a sense of inner calm amidst the external digital chaos. □□==Key Takeaways

Integrating mindfulness in your technological journeys promises a transformative shift from Digital Chaos to Digital Calm. This journey is not about surrendering technology; it's about embracing it on healthier, more constructive terms. Just as a seasoned pianist creates the exquisite symphony by taming chaos of keys, the right digital habits can harmonize technology's immense potential with our deep-seated need for peace and tranquility. Allowing mindfulness to navigate your digital conduct will be an empowering journey, filled with revelations, healthier habits, and a renewed sense of self amidst the digital cosmos.

Chapter 7. Recognizing and Managing Digital Stressors

Stress, in one form or another, is an unavoidable part of everyday life. And while some stressors may originate from our offline environments, the increasing amount of time that we spend online is leading to a new host of rattling antagonisms: digital stressors. Here we delve into the recognition and management of digital stressors.

7.1. Identifying Digital Stressors

The first and perhaps most crucial step in managing the onslaught of digital-age obstacles is recognizing what these digital stressors look like. They can be as explicit as cyberbullying or as inconspicuous as a subtly intimidating email. Here are some of the most common digital stressors:

- **Information Overload:** With an overabundance of information available online, the task of processing and understanding it all becomes increasingly stressful.

- **Cyberbullying:** Malicious actions taken against individuals on digital platforms.

- **Phantom Vibrations Syndrome:** The perception that your phone is vibrating or ringing when it's not.

- **Nomophobia:** A term coined to represent the fear of being without your mobile phone.

- **Social Expectation & Comparison:** The pressure to portray an idealized life online, leading to stress and anxiety.

- **Fear of Missing Out (FOMO):** The angst that an exciting or interesting event may currently be happening elsewhere.

7.2. Relationships with Digital Platforms

In recognizing these stressors, we need to take into account our relationships with different digital platforms. Each platform creates unique forms of interactions, and these interactions can differentiate the stressors we encounter. Some platforms may emphasize personal comparison and fear of FOMO, such as Instagram, while others, like Twitter, may elicit situations of information overload and contentious discourse.

Understanding the unique ways in which each platform triggers stressors for you personally is also important. People react to and process things differently; what may be a stressor for one person, may not be for another. Hold a mindful lens to your digital experience and observe how the different elements of the digital world affect you.

7.3. Digital Detox

Since digital stress triggers can often be relentless, making time for a 'digital detox' can be incredibly beneficial. This involves intentionally setting aside time to disconnect from digital devices and recognizing the importance of establishing digital boundaries in promoting personal well-being.

Here are some ways to implement a digital detox:

- Set dedicated times in the day to disconnect from all digital devices.
- Establish device-free zones in your living space, like the bedroom or dining area.
- Use tech tools that promote focus and a clutter-free digital environment.

- Explore hobbies and interests that encourage you to spend time away from screens.

- Enforce "No Device" periods, such as the first hour after waking up and the last hour before bed.

7.4. Mindfulness Practices

Where a digital detox provides an 'external' management plan for digital stressors, mindfulness approaches the issue from an 'internal' perspective. Mindfulness, at its core, is the practice of purposefully focusing our attention on the present moment and accepting it without judgment.

Try these mindfulness practices:

- **Mindful Breathing:** This practice involves focusing your entire attention on your breath as it flows in and out of your body.

- **Sensory Observation:** Engage fully with your sensory experiences in a given moment – what you're seeing, hearing, smelling, tasting, and feeling.

- **Emotional Awareness:** Observe your emotions impartially, acknowledging without necessarily changing or supressing them.

- **Mindful Listening:** Instead of passively hearing, take notice of the sounds, rhythms, and silences around you with a beginner's mind, as though for the first time.

- **Body Scan:** Involves systematically paying attention to different parts of your body, from your toes to your head.

Resultant of mindfulness, you can foster more healthy, aware, and balanced relationship with digital interactions.

7.5. Seeking Professional Help

It is important to remember that help is always available. If digital stressors are impacting your health and well-being, it is crucial to reach out to professionals who can provide guidance, such as therapists or psychologists specializing in digital stress or other mental health issues brought on by digital technology.

Understanding, acknowledging, and addressing digital stressors can guide us towards a healthier balance in our digital lives. With diligent application of the lessons provided here, one can transition from experiencing online platforms as potential fields of psychological minefields to landscapes of conscious presence and calm. Remember, in the realm of the digital world, mastering your interactions is the key to cultivating better mental health.

Chapter 8. Mindful Social Media: Creating a Positive Digital Experience

Social media, once a groundbreaking novelty, has become part and parcel of our everyday lives. However, with its rapid evolution, the collective consciousness of giving and receiving information has fundamentally shifted. The consequence? A plethora of emotional and mental health implications that can range from mild to severe. This isn't a crisis, but rather an opportunity to approach social media from a perspective of mindfulness, transforming it into an oasis of positivity and balance in the hustle and bustle of the digital world.

8.1. Understanding the Digital Landscape

To begin, we need to understand the digital landscape. Social media platforms, including Facebook, Instagram, Twitter, and their ilk, have narrative structures that allow for active participation, engagement, and collaboration. As the lines between reality and the virtual blur, our experiences on these platforms progressively echo our everyday lives, creating an interconnected world that can be both beautiful and overwhelming.

The virtual interactions, validations, disapprovals, and relationships we experience on these platforms often set a tone for our emotions, affecting not just the way we interact with the digital world but also how we perceive ourselves and the physical environment around us. Being mindful of these influences can act as a cornerstone towards crafting a healthier digital experience.

8.2. The Power of Mindfulness

First, let's understand mindfulness. In the words of Jon Kabat-Zin, a prominent mindfulness pioneer, mindfulness means "paying attention in a particular way: on purpose, in the present moment, and nonjudgmentally." When integrated into our digital experiences, mindfulness cultivates a sense of self-awareness that allows us to consciously control our social media behaviour, rather than getting swept away in the reactive, incessant tide of updates, posts, likes, shares, and comments.

An emphatic approach to mindful social media incorporates both mindful usage and mindful consumption. By fostering mindful presence, the practice empowers us to control our reactions and responses to various digital stimuli and make thoughtful decisions on the content we expose ourselves to online.

8.3. Mindful Usage of Social Media

Mindful usage is essentially the approach of cultivating consciousness around why, how, when, and what we communicate through social media. The first step is to identify the driving forces behind our social media engagement. Ask yourself: Am I seeking validation? Trying to escape boredom? Looking for amusement or social connection? By recognizing our intent, we can better navigate our digital interactions.

Equally important is adopting a mindful posture towards the content we share online. Before posting, retweeting, or sharing content, pause and think: Is what I'm sharing helpful? Is it necessary or respectful? Does it represent my values? Such a conscious approach not only benefits our personal well-being but also contributes to a more positive and healthier digital environment.

It's also important to pay attention to when and how often we use social media. Checking social media as the first thing in the morning, for instance, can set a tone for the day, affecting our mood, productivity, and interactions. One possible strategy to manage the time spent online is to establish designated "digital-free" times, wherein we steer clear from our devices and engage with the physical world around us.

8.4. Mindful Consumption of Digital Content

Just as mindful usage focuses on our actions and behaviours, mindful consumption is about controlling what we let into our digital consciousness. The constantly updating feeds, virality, and information overload make it easy to indiscriminately consume content, which can unknowingly affect our mental equanimity.

Start by auditing your digital environment. Unfollow, mute, or block content that leaves you feeling negative, anxious, or unsettled. Cultivate a feed that reflects your values, boosts positivity, and enriches your life. You can also employ beneficial tools and features offered by social media platforms, like "see less of this" or "hide post," to tailor your digital exposure.

Besides content quality, being aware of content quantity is equally essential. Digital detox or breaks from the relentless information influx does not mean completely eliminating digital consumption but emphasizes establishing a healthier and more balanced digital diet.

8.5. Cultivating Mindful Connections

Reconditioning our social media habits is not an overnight task. But by gradually incorporating mindfulness in our daily digital interactions, we can transform social media into a tool of empowerment that nurtures our mental well-being. Cultivate digital relationships that are meaningful; engage in conversations that are constructive and respectful. Limit your exposure to negative discourses and embrace connections that share a common sense of positivity.

8.6. Conclusion: Towards a Mindful Digital Culture

Our relationship with social media is intricately woven into our lives, influencing our emotional and mental health. Developing a mindful approach to our social media usage can revolutionize this interaction, leading to a more positive and healthier digital experience.

Echoing the words of Zen master Thich Nhat Hanh, "The next Buddha may well be a Sangha," it's an affectionate and profound reminder that our combined conscious efforts can shape our digital culture. In this shared digital universe, fostering mindfulness is not an individual journey alone; it is a collective stride towards a healthier, more positive, and inclusive digital world. Let's embrace this journey wholeheartedly because the path to digital mindfulness begins with us.

Chapter 9. Building Mindful Relationships with Technology

Diving deep into our digital lives begins with a fundamental shift in our understanding: that, like in real life, our relationships with technology in the digital sphere require mindfulness, careful curating and diligent discipline. While this concept may seem foreboding, in reality it is a path paved with enlightening perspectives, awareness, and emotional liberation.

9.1. Defining Mindful Relationships with Technology

A mindful relationship with technology does not mean we shun the digital world altogether. Contrarily, it implies a balanced approach where we remain alert and aware during interactions within cyberspace, maintaining our focus and mental well-being. It enables us to shift from being passive recipients of content to becoming mindful consumers, creators, and sharers of digital information.

From this perspective, we can start understanding technology as a neutral entity, a tool that can either serve or hinder us depending on our approach and usage.

9.2. Understanding Digital Well-Being

Digital well-being is a term that has been gaining recognition in recent times, essentially reflecting our mental and emotional state when interacting with digital technologies. It necessitates understanding the impact of our digital behaviors on our overall health, relationships, productivity, and even our quality of sleep.

To assess your digital well-being, consider how often you feel the need to check your device, how long you spend on various digital channels, and how you feel afterward. Do these digital interactions make you feel anxious or content, drained or rejuvenated?

By gaining awareness of these aspects, we arm ourselves with the knowledge to mold our digital interactions to better match our personal needs and boundaries, thus facilitating a healthier digital lifestyle.

9.3. Practical Steps for Building Mindful Relationships with Technology

Mindful use of technology is not just an abstract idea, but a pragmatically achievable intention set in actions. Let's explore some measures you can adopt to enhance your mindfulness:

1. **Digital Audit:** Reflect on how your digital activities affect your well-being. Are they aligning with your personal and professional goals, or are they distressing you?

2. **Mindful Notifications:** Consider reducing the number of notifications you receive, encouraging a more intentional and less distracted use of your digital devices.

3. **Digital Detox:** Incorporate periods of digital abstinence into your routine – These could be certain hours of the day, or full days, depending on your comfort and feasibility.

4. **Purposeful Digital Interactions:** Use your devices for purposeful interactions which are in sync with your life goals and perspectives.

9.4. Devices as Tools, Not Masters

Remember, your digital devices are tools, and you are their master. Choose to use technology as a means for growth and knowledge, rather than letting it dominate your day and your well-being.

One effective way of doing this is by practicing mindful presence when you use your devices. Before engaging, ask yourself: What is my intention with this device right now? Do I need to check my emails, or am I just aimlessly exploring the digital landscape? By understanding your 'why,' you can better dictate your 'how.'

9.5. The Space between Stimulus and Response

Renowned psychiatrist and Holocaust survivor, Dr. Viktor Frankl, wrote, "Between stimulus and response there is a space. In that space is our power to choose our response. In our response lies our growth and our freedom."

This concept is at the cornerstone of building a mindful relationship with technology. Our devices, with incessant notifications and constant updates, are designed to provoke immediate, almost reflexive responses. When you learn to briefly pause and respond mindfully, you gain control over your digital interactions, rather than succumb to automated reflexes.

As we walk this path, we find that our mindful relationship with technology can greatly impact other areas of our lives too: relationships, performance at work, and even our mental health. By approaching technology through the lens of mindfulness, we are not only helping ourselves but also setting a positive example for others to follow.

If this mindful movement gains momentum, just imagine the

potential! An Internet where every interaction is respect-filled, every piece of content enriches, and every reciprocal action blooms from a place of awareness and intention. A utopia? Perhaps. But one that begins with our first mindful click, swipe, or scroll. This is the sunrise of mindfulness in the digital era. And what a beautiful dawn it promises to be.

In summary, setting a mindful relationship with technology allows us to command our devices and the digital realm it accesses, rather than being dictated by them. It coincides with cultivating a healthier, richer digital experience conducive to overall well-being. As we move ahead in our journey, let's remember: the tool should not overmaster the user. In the realm of technology, each click, swipe, or scroll has the potential for mindful awareness. Become a part of this movement and revolutionize your digital reality!

Chapter 10. Strategies for Mindfulness: Enhancing Online Experiences

Mindfulness is more than simply a buzzword. It's a profound practice of bringing conscious attention to our experiences in the present moment, and it has the power to transform our relationship with our digital tools.

Digital mindfulness enables us to gain control over our digital lives, helping us to understand and manage our online behavior. As we become more conscious of how we interact with technology, we become better equipped to integrate thoughtful patterns of use that align with our broader values and mental health needs.

10.1. The Intersection of Mindfulness and Technology

Understanding mindfulness in a digital context begins with recognizing the complexities inherent to technology's role in our lives. While digital platforms provide numerous benefits, they also present potential distractions, stressors, and threats to mental health. To foster a healthier digital environment, it's crucial to harness the power of mindfulness, adapting ancient wisdom for contemporary challenges.

Applying mindfulness to our online experiences can involve various techniques and strategies, all of which aim to promote conscious use of digital technology.

10.2. Contrasting Mindless Scrolling and Mindful Surfing

One of the first steps in encouraging a mindful digital experience involves shifting from mindless scrolling to mindful surfing. Mindless scrolling often leads to feelings of disconnection, loneliness, and an overwhelming influx of information. In contrast, mindful surfing means leveraging digital platforms with intention and focus, engaging with content that genuinely resonates with our interests and values.

Transitioning towards this mindful approach involves being aware of our online activities and adopting healthy habits like setting time restrictions for screen use, utilizing the DND (Do Not Disturb) mode, and consciously choosing to engage with uplifting digital content.

10.3. Cultivating Conscious Connections

Building meaningful relationships online extends beyond scrolling through an endless feed of updates. It's about nurturing associations that encourage positivity, growth, and genuine interaction.

Engaging mindfully with online communities and networks can involve steps like limiting the number of people we follow to those who truly inspire or educate us, periodically auditing our friend lists, and partaking in uplifting digital experiences like webinars, online retreats, or digital workshops.

10.4. Being Present Online

Though it may seem counterintuitive in an environment often characterized by multi-layered media and rapid-fire updates, it's possible to be fully "present" in our online experience. Practicing mindfulness when engaging online can involve concentrated effort to single-tasking - focusing on one application, conversation, or task at a time instead of succumbing to the pull of multitasking.

10.5. Mindful Notifications

Notifications are fundamental to digital experience, but they can often lead to distraction and stress when not managed mindfully. Tools such as customizing notification settings, scheduling 'quiet hours,' and using mindfulness reminders can all facilitate more mindful interactions with this aspect of our digital lives.

10.6. The Value of Digital Detox

Digital detox – specified periods of time without digital devices – is a powerful strategy for fostering mindfulness. These detox periods provide space to develop an appreciation for our offline world and to reflect on the kind of digital life we aim to cultivate. Integrating regular digital detox periods into our routine can encourage more mindful engagement when we do interact with our devices.

10.7. Mindfulness Apps and Digital Well-being Tools

There are many apps and digital tools specifically designed to support mindfulness, from meditation apps like Headspace and Insight Timer, to digital wellness tools like Forest, which fosters focus, or RescueTime, which tracks time spent on different applications and websites.

10.8. Media and Mindfulness

Mindfulness also extends to how we consume media online. This can involve choosing to consume media that nurtures positivity, evolving our media choices in alignment with our personal growth and values, and practicing conscious consumption - noticing how different types of media impact our mood and mental state.

Each strategy or technique isn't a magical solution alone, but collectively, they can contribute significantly to ensuring mindful, conscious use of digital spaces. It takes dedication and practice to develop new, healthier patterns of digital engagement, but the resulting resilience, tranquility, and understanding can certainly transform our experience of the digital world, leading to enhanced mental health.

In a world where technology is deeply integrated into every facet of life, digital mindfulness is no longer merely an option; it's a need. We encourage you to take these insights and strategies forward as you continue your exploration of digital mindfulness and its profound implications for digital health, well-being, and the quality of life in our ever-evolving digital age.

Chapter 11. Digital Detox: The Healthy Break You Need

In an era infused with technology, it's easy to feel fatigued and overwhelmed. Scrolling through messages, squinting at screens, constantly being bound to notifications - this digital deluge can drain us hollow while secluding us from our core humanity. This space elicits the need for a 'Digital Detox,' a conscious choice to shun screens temporarily, stripping off the digital veneer, and embracing a subtler resonance with self, rejuvenating our mental health.

11.1. Understanding the Digital Detox

A digital detox refers to a period when an individual refrains from using digital devices such as smartphones, computers, tablets, social media platforms and digital television, to reduce stress, focus on real-life social interactions, and reconnect with the inner self. It is like hitting a 'Reset' button for your brain, providing a chance to salvage and nurture mental and emotional well-being. It's a concept grounded in both simplicity and necessity, a timely intervention amid our accelerated digital engagement.

11.2. The Need for a Digital Detox

Digital devices, as indispensable as they've become to our everyday living, have undeniably ushered in a slew of mental health challenges. Anxiety, stress, depression, decreased productivity, sleep disturbances, and a diminished sense of self-worth are some of the dark shadows the digital revolution casts.

Research underscores the harmful effects of excessive screen time and digital engagement on mental health. A 2018 study in the Journal of Social and Clinical Psychology found a significant decrease in loneliness and depression among participants who limited their social media usage compared to a control group. Another review in the journal BMC Psychiatry revealed a significant association between longer screen time and anxiety and depression, particularly among adolescents and young adults.

This is where the idea of digital detox becomes crucial. We need a well-deserved break from this relentless digital consumption, an avenue to reclaim control over our digital lives and nourish mental peace.

11.3. Embarking on a Digital Detox Journey

Deciding to undertake a digital detox represents the first step towards this endeavor. A successful detox requires setting clear and realistic goals, carefully planning, and adopting a disciplined approach. Here are some steps to help guide your path:

1. Train Yourself for the Detox: You cannot achieve a full detox overnight. It's advisable to begin by limiting usage and progressively down-scaling your digital even further.

2. Set Clear Boundaries: Specific goals can ease this transition. Designate tech-free zones at home, establish 'no screen' hours, or vow to check your social media only once a day.

3. Prepare for Challenges: Disconnecting may lead to withdrawal symptoms—restlessness, irritation, or discomfort. Anticipate these and face them mindfully.

4. Engage in Other Activities: Fill the void left by digital devices with engaging non-digital activities such as reading, gardening, spending time with loved ones, or practicing meditation.

5. Stay Committed: Temporary cravings may veer you off course. Staying committed to your goal is vital. Take each day as it comes, celebrating small victories along the way.

11.4. Post Detox: Making Mindful Connections

Completing a digital detox is a commendable feat, but the real challenge lies in embedding these practices into daily life. The aim is not to reject digital outright but to foster a healthier relationship with it. It's about using technology with intention and purpose, not letting it become a compulsive habit or an emotional crutch.

Consider mindful technology use, where you're entirely present, engaged, and conscious of the effects of your online activity. This might involve checking emails in designated times, consciously choosing to not respond immediately to every notification, or using apps that encourage mindfulness and healthy behavior.

Remember, everyone's detox journey will look different, and it's okay. The ultimate goal is to shift from 'being digitally distracted' to 'being digitally mindful,' laying the foundation for better mental health.

11.5. The Rippling Effects of Digital Detox on Mental Health

Reducing screen time and regulating digital consumption has profound implications on psychological health. A digital detox can lead to improved sleep, reduced anxiety and depression, better physical health, heightened productivity, enhanced creativity, stronger real-life relationships, and an overall improved quality of life.

The effects transcend the individual level. They can ripple into societal dynamics, giving way to a more compassionate, empathetic, and connected world, where technology is used as a tool for enhancement rather than a source of depletion.

Digital detox doesn't seek to vilify technology but kindle a mindful approach. As we master the art of balancing our online-offline lives, nurturing our mental health, we will realize that the digital realm need not be a hall of clattering chaos but a canvas to paint our stories, reflecting our humanity, not eroding it. Let this detox be your compass to navigate the convoluted corners of the digital world, guiding you towards a life of clarity, peace, and mindful connections. Embrace the detox- Not as a rigid rulebook, but as a graceful dance between the digital and the human, syncing tech engagement with mental tranquility.

Chapter 12. The Future of Digital Mindfulness: What Comes Next?

As we delve deeper into the 21st-century, it is inexorable that we will continue to engage with digital platforms with a higher frequency and intensity. The key question that confronts us, then, is how we can better adapt digital practices to be more desirable for our inner selves and mental health. The answer lies not in the vain attempt to shun digital technology, but in fostering a mindful attitude towards it- in every click, every notification, every scroll.

12.1. Cognizing the Need for Digital Mindfulness

The future of digital mindfulness begins when we acknowledge the importance of harnessing digital technology in a mindful way. This means being fully present and engaged while interacting with digital platforms, rather than mindlessly scrolling through our feeds.

Such cognizance is increasingly important as we journey further into the digital age. As the world pivots toward a digital future, our interaction with technology is becoming more immersive. Virtual Reality(VR) and Augmented Reality(AR) technologies are stepping stones towards a future where the lines between the digital and physical world may blur. However, they also provide a potential platform for mindful engagement. Mindful VR experiences are already being developed, allowing users to step into peaceful, immersive environments to meditate and relax.

12.2. A Shift towards Intentional Design

Central to the future of digital mindfulness is the concept of intentional design. The way digital platforms are designed can significantly impact how we engage with them.

Many tech firms are now recognizing this and are providing features enabling digital wellbeing. For instance, many smartphones now have "Do Not Disturb" and "Night Shift" features. Apps like "Forest" gamify focus and productivity, encouraging users to put down their phones and concentrate on their work or a physical book.

However, the push for more mindful digital experiences is not limited to screen time reduction. Efforts are being made to make our digital interactions more meaningful and less stressful. For instance, platforms are experimenting with hiding 'like' counts and comments to reduce social pressure.

12.3. Mindful Artificial Intelligence

Artificial intelligence (AI) will play a crucial role in shaping the future of digital mindfulness. AI's in-depth learning capabilities can provide personalized mindful experiences, pushing notifications at the right time, suggesting breaks, or even guiding a tailored meditation session.

Moreover, future AI could assist in recognizing patterns in our digital behavior that may be detrimental to our mental health. This capability could enable AI to alert us or suggest healthier digital habits, making mindfulness an integral part of our online routine.

12.4. Education and Digital Literacy

A key aspect of our digital mindfulness future involves an informed and literate user base. It is crucial to empower individuals with the knowledge and tools to navigate the digital world mindfully.

This involves a shift in how we teach digital literacy, with an emphasis not just on practical skills but also on understanding the psychological impact of digital behaviors. Making digital mindfulness a component of the larger digital literacy narrative is essential for a healthier digital society.

12.5. The Role of Legislation and Policy

Just as legislation plays a key role in controlling the excesses in other sectors, it will be vital in shaping the landscape of digital mindfulness. To date, there has been sporadic regulation in this sphere, with laws focusing on individual aspects like data privacy or cyberbullying.

In the future, we may see comprehensive legislation that promotes mindfulness and mental wellbeing in the digital sphere. Tech companies may be required to integrate mindful design principles, and educational institutions may be mandated to include digital mindfulness in their curricula.

12.6. The Holistic Journey

The future isn't about a singular solution or a magic button that instantly resolves the issues with our digital lifestyle. It's a holistic journey involving changes in behaviors, norms, and systems. A conscious effort to learn, unlearn, and relearn habits is required to nurture a mindful digital experience.

As each of us embarks on this journey towards digital mindfulness, we have the potential to transform not just our own mental wellbeing, but the digital society as a whole. In the future of digital mindfulness, technology is not the antagonist but a companion and tool to foster tranquility and mental health.

The journey is far from easy, but with every passing day, we are getting closer to a world where digital mindfulness isn't a concept, but a norm. Our devices and platforms have the potential to become tools of tranquility, fostering instead of hindering mental health, when governed by mindful practices and norms. The future is bright and hopeful, and as we move towards it, let's bring along our mindfulness into this digital age.

www.ingramcontent.com/pod-product-compliance
Lightning Source LLC
LaVergne TN
LVHW051626050326
832903LV00033B/4677